In their matching US Refugee Program sweatshirts and white canvas shoes (above), it is a sad night for these Lost Boys—the last night they will be in Africa, the only land they have ever known. Many of them, faced with leaving lifelong friends behind in Kakuma, spent their last few hours crying and taking their last deep breaths of the cool African night, while grasping pictures of those whom they were leaving. Others sat silently on hard plastic airport chairs, arms folded, frightened to death of what they would face in a new mysterious land. The rest of the group were in smiles immersed in an in-depth debate over the proper way to use a toilet and how to remain alive when one comes in contact with a thing known as snow—all things that the boys still had no comprehension of even with the orientation given to them before they left Kakuma. No matter how they dealt with leaving, each would step aboard that plane to New York via Brussels, about to embark on a life journey.

As the refugees continue to arrive and leave, there remains one constant of Kakuma, the Turkana (right and following page). They have inhabited this land for centuries, but it is questionable how long this ancient culture can sustain itself in an ever-encroaching world.

Lost Boys (above) huddle around the posting of names that will be the next group of boys headed to the US. Their lives and future stop in time as each approaches the board hoping to find his name. This process begins with an initial screening by the UNHCR. After that a Lost Boy goes through three interviews by the JVA which inquires about the screening, personal history and casework concerning the trek from Sudan to Ethiopia to Kenya. If all statements and inquiries prove to be acceptable they are then sent to a final meeting with the INS. All casework will then be reviewed and the questions asked during the JVA interview are repeated to assure that the specific Lost Boy is the correct case on file. If all goes well, the final step is an orientation by the Immigration Organization of Migration (IOM), which is responsible for transportation of the Lost Boys and attempts to prepare them for the US.

The enactment of the USA P2 resettlement initiative has also been important. This called for the resettlement opportunity for a majority of the original Lost Boys who reached Kakuma between 1992 and 1994 to come live in the US. This step was looked at by some as a kind invitation to the boys who have suffered through pure hell, to enjoy a peaceful and prosperous life in the United States. Others see it as a public relations stunt to make the US look good, while ignoring the atrocities and human rights abuses in Sudan. Both sides can be debated, but the reality was that in November 2000 the Lost Boys began the last leg of their epic journey, coming to America. To complete this trek they would not have to run from soldiers or hide from bombings. They would have to endure a process of interviews, which would be nothing in comparison to previous challenges.

Mother and child (far right) experienced their first flight. Her son, suffering from severe tuberculosis, is being transferred to Nairobi via UNHCR aircraft to receive medical attention. Kakuma Refugee Camp uses a referral system to send refugee patients to the local Kakuma Mission Hospital, Lodwar District Hospital, Lokichokio ICRC or to Nairobi, according to the severity of each case.

Several new arrivals from the International Committee of the Red Cross in Lokichokio (left), showed off their battle wounds. Their bandages covered bullet wounds. They have experienced irreversible psychological damage as child soldiers for the SPLA. Their ages ranged from thirteen to seventeen years old.

The older Lost Boys (above) are preparing for resettlement and pass the time enjoying their favorite form of recreation, soccer.

Not all are so fortunate, however. A young Sudanese Dinka Bor man (following pages) lay dead from what appeared to be a gunshot wound to the head along with several machete blows. This is only one of the several who lay dead in and around the riverbed after fighting arose in Kakuma. The altercation was explained as a water dispute, then as an argument about a girl, but everyone knew all too well that it was political. There is a UNHCR mandate against any political activity in the camp. With such a large refugee

population it is nearly impossible to enforce this rule. The true reason for the fighting was an inter-fractional dispute within the SPLA between the Dinka Bor and Dinka Bahr-el-Ghazal tribes in Sudan only days previous to the fighting in the camp.

News of divisions in Sudan travels quickly to Kakuma by either word of mouth or radio contact inside the camp. Fighting like this had occurred before in the camp, but this was the first instance where the use of AK-47's were present. Sudanese refugee communities were displaced within Kakuma. The very place where they had sought refuge had now turned into the war zone they fled.

While fleeing military attack from the north, the South Sudanese themselves have also been responsible for human rights violations and violence against one another when ancient tribal or political feuding flares. It is a constant concern in the close confinement of the camp.

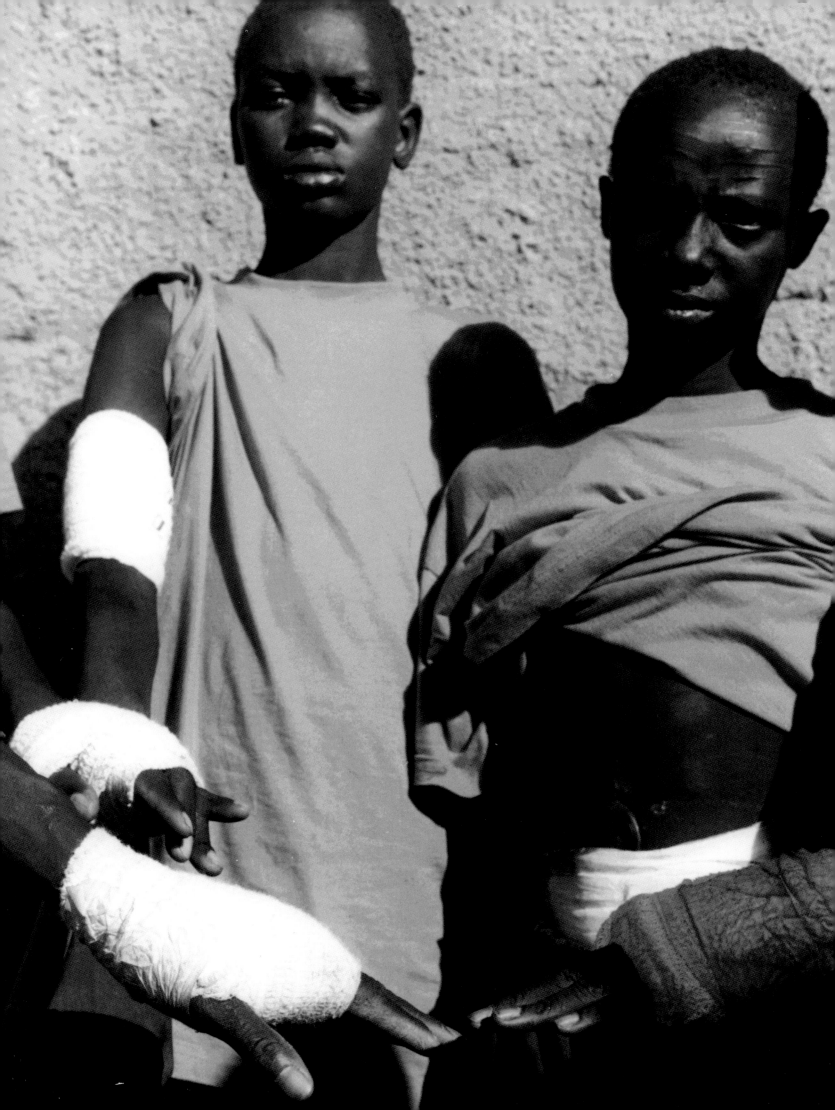

Lost Boys (previous pages) wait in line to attend interviews by the Joint Volunteer Agency. Each boy will attend a total of three meetings by the JVA, a critical step for resettlement in the US. Originally in 1992, there were 7000 Lost Boys that entered Kakuma without any family.

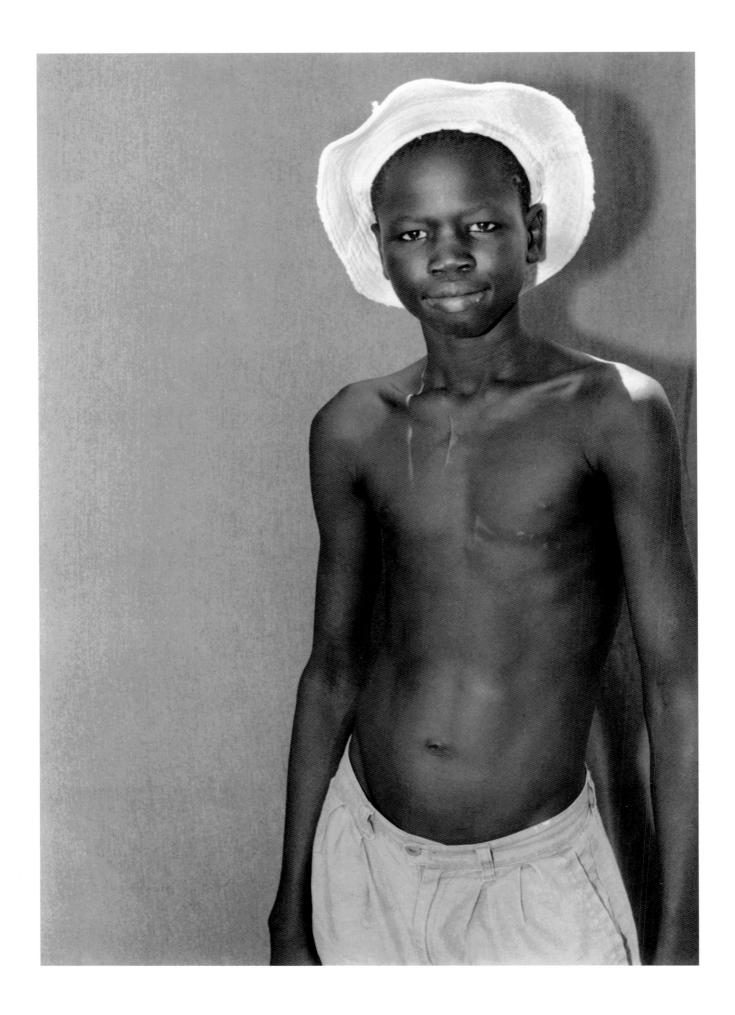

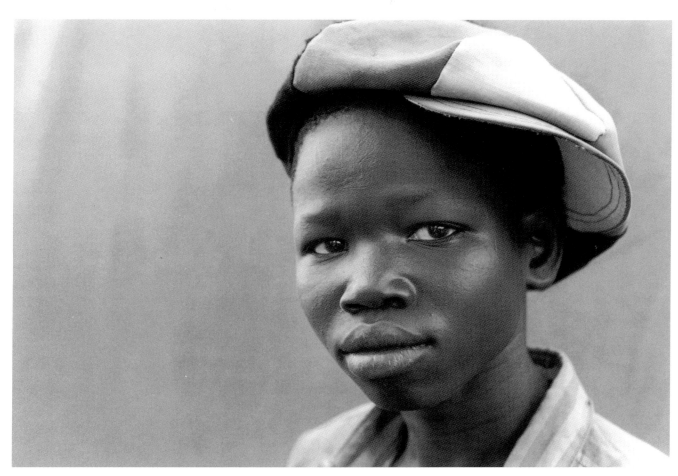

These two young men and the two on the preceding pages are among the original Lost Boys who reached the camp between 1992 and 1994. The boy on the previous page is holding his only possession from his homeland in Sudan. His cherished Bible has made the journey with him through the battlegrounds of Sudan, Ethiopia and now to Kenya's Kakuma Refugee Camp.

The boys survived the war and famine of their countries, but the boy above bears the scars of his bout with measles.

Their brothers, sisters and cousins who rode on their backs as they walked hundreds of miles to try to reach safety, are now the age the Lost Boys were when they first entered the camp. Some, portrayed on the following pages, are now in their teens. Because of their young age they are not the ones being resettled to the U.S. It is extremely difficult to deal with the loss of their brothers who protected them and brought them to Kakuma.

Service (INS) as part of a US State Department mandate. In the next several years the remaining original Lost Boys will join their brothers in the US, while a new generation takes their place in Kakuma.

The Lost Boys over the past several years have taken me in as one of their own, willing to share what little food they had and just as willing to share their personal stories of great tragedy. Countless hours have been spent huddled up in a small hut, sharing laughter and tears with them. I sat and listened to their stories, each as heart-wrenching as the other. These young men are among the greatest examples of human triumph, yet they would be the first to disagree.

I was saddened that this was likely to be my last trip to Kakuma for quite a while. I didn't know how to say good-bye to my lost brothers. My final days in the camp were spent with them in their huts like we had spent so many days before, but it was now time to leave. The realization of not seeing them again hit me as I flew over the camp for one last time and saw a group of them on their soccer fields. They began to grow more and more faint as our small aircraft disappeared into the clouds.

After reaching Nairobi, I rested for several days, cleared up matters with the UNHCR and said my good-byes and thanks to friends. It was the usual cool Kenyan night when I made my way to the airport to head home. I got my boarding pass and went to the waiting area.

There they were: a tall, slender ragtag group of Lost Boys. Something like this could not have been scripted any better. They had just been cleared to leave Kakuma for America. I was greeted with smiles and hugs from my lost brothers. I don't know who was happier to see each other, them or me. It was hard for me not to laugh. They looked like a professional basketball team with their matching sweatshirts and slacks and white canvas shoes. I sat with the group of thirty or so and just laughed. Many of them were eager to tell me of their first ride in an airplane, which they took from Kakuma to Nairobi. Others wanted to share with me their first experience of taking a shower in the hotel they stayed in the previous night. The laughter broke when one of the Lost Boys wrapped his long lanky arms around me as tears fell from his face. After the boy finally let go I could see that it was DM. Deng James Majue was

one of the Lost Boys who had become a close friend. I tried to console him, but who was I to tell him not to be afraid? That wasn't the case. We began talking and he told me of the guilt he felt leaving behind all those in Kakuma. As we sat in the airport together he told me, "My tomorrow is assured, but theirs is not." What he told me reminded me of my interview with him in December 1999, one of my first with any of the Lost Boys, and one of the most horrific.

"The soldiers came from everywhere. They were not asking for SPLA. They were just killing. I was not in the village when they came. I saw smoke in the village so I ran to find my family. I heard gunshots. Many were running. The huts were on fire. One lady who lived near us told me to run. Not to go to the village. They would kill me. She yelled at me to run the other way. I saw one woman running with her baby. She was shot and dropped her baby . . . then they shot the baby. So then I ran too. I kept running for many days, but soon I could run no longer. I did not eat for many days. I then had to walk, I was too weak to run anymore. Many of the people who walked with me died. Sometimes their children would die. Sometimes they would die. There was no food for any of us. We were suffering. Sometimes we would eat plants and grass if we found it. Sometimes when we passed villages we could get food. But sometimes there were no villages.

"Many of us walking had been separated from our families. We don't know if they had been killed. We don't know when we will be killed. Sometimes we see airplanes in the sky. One time it dropped many bombs. It killed my good friend. We had to run away from the soldiers so they don't kill us. Sometimes lion kill us. One time one boy died from disease. Then they took his clothes. Some boys said to eat him. We had no food for many days and they wanted to eat him. I don't want that. Some boys fighting so they don't eat him. But they say they must or they will die too. I don't know if they eat him . . . I still walked and did not want to watch. Sometimes I wish that I was dead. I have no drink or nothing to eat. I have no family with me. Sometimes I want to die then. When I was walking I don't think of tomorrow. You don't even know if there was to be a tomorrow. You only think of today. Now I am happy because I can think that there will be tomorrow."

THE LOST BOYS

Named by a journalist after the group of orphans led by Peter Pan, the Lost Boys of Sudan have endured and survived a life of suffering far from any fairy tale. The Lost Boys and I have spent endless hours in their huts together, they towering over me with scarred foreheads and pulled teeth signifying their passage into manhood, each of them reliving and sharing their experiences of utter horror and triumph.

It began in 1987, with Islamic law having been established in Sudan only years before. The Christians and animists of the South refused to have Islam enforced on them. The SPLA took up an armed resistance against the Islamic government in the north and has been engaged in a war ever since. The Arab government began bombing campaigns and used a ground force of soldiers and government-backed militias to carry out acts of genocide on all Black animists and Christians of the South. Young boys, looking after herds in remote cattle camps as is the tradition in South Sudan, were away from their villages during the attacks and bombings. Most who survived were orphaned or separated from their families when their villages were destroyed. There was an exodus of monumental proportion. Thousands upon thousands of South Sudanese—the majority of whom were young boys—fled for their lives. It was the beginning of an epic journey.

These Lost Boys began walking, many of them having no clue to where. Sudan is the largest country in Africa, a quarter of the size of the United States, and the Lost Boys would need to walk over 1000 miles to safety. In the weeks and months of their journeys, traveling mostly at night to avoid being bombed from the air or captured by ground troops, lions were a constant threat. The boys began to form close-knit groups, a new sense of family following the loss of their own. They traveled across Saharan desert, into jungles, over mountains and through swamps—all studded with land mines. Most walked barefoot.

It was at refugee camps across the border in Ethiopia that they thought they would finally find peace, but they had to cross the crocodile-infested Gilo River to get there. Thousands drowned because they could not swim. Eventually some 33,000 Lost Boys reached the three camps.

Many of the young Sudanese refugees remained in the camps for four hard years enduring famine and disease. Then a coup of the Mengistu government in 1991 forced the boys out of Ethiopia and across the dreaded Gilo River at flood stage, Ethiopian militia shooting at them from behind. They headed back into the heated civil war that inflamed their homeland, the very reason they had left.

About 13,000 Lost Boys searched for yet another place of safety. This would prove to be even more dangerous than their initial trek to Ethiopia. Now they were hunted by Ethiopian soldiers, Sudanese government militias and soldiers, as well as SPLA rebel forces trying to capture the young boys to add them to their rebel resistance soldiers.

Somehow, 7000 Lost Boys managed to survive and reach the newly opened Kakuma Refugee Camp in Kenya in 1992. Here they found shelter, food, education and safety. Once in the camp, 2000 Lost Boys under the age of twelve were placed in foster care within the refugee community. The remaining boys were put into huts of five boys per household, according to the close bonds they had built. All the boys had left was each other.

Five adolescent boys in a ten-by-ten-foot mud hut—three boys lie on makeshift beds and the extra two boys sleep on the floor, sharing a small pot of cornmeal between them daily. Each night they share candlelight and take turns using the same pen to review each other's school work. Along with having an unbridled passion for religion and academics, each has a gentle politeness.

No longer boys, they have grown to young men. Most are now between the ages of eighteen and thirty years old. It is now time for them to make one more journey. It is an emotional time of good-byes as the original and very first refugees of Kakuma now depart. Since November 2000 over 3500 Lost Boys have been resettled from New York City to Phoenix, by the US Immigration and Naturalization

A Catholic priest's outstretched hands (previous page) feed the mouth of a Turkana at Easter Mass. First contact with non-Africans was made with the Turkana in 1960. Due to extreme drought and famine, the Catholic Mission brought aid and religion to this remote region. The Turkana welcomed missionaries with open arms as long as the aid came with them. Missionaries brought a Bible in the Turkana's native language. This made many of them feel the Bible was made especially for the Turkana, but they simply hadn't discovered it yet. It was the first introduction of an outside religion into this traditional society. A mission hospital has been built and several other social services are provided by Catholic Relief Services and the Catholic Mission. Still, many Turkana remain wary of this new religion, while others combine both Catholicism and their traditional animist beliefs.

A new arrival (above) holds the two most precious things she owns, her child and her cross. These are the only things she carried as she fled her homeland of Sudan. She also said that these are the two reasons why she left her country, so her child would grow up in safety and she could practice her belief in Christianity without fear.

This church leader (right) proudly displays his passion for Christianity as he parades and preaches throughout the camp on Easter Sunday, while other church members march (following pages).

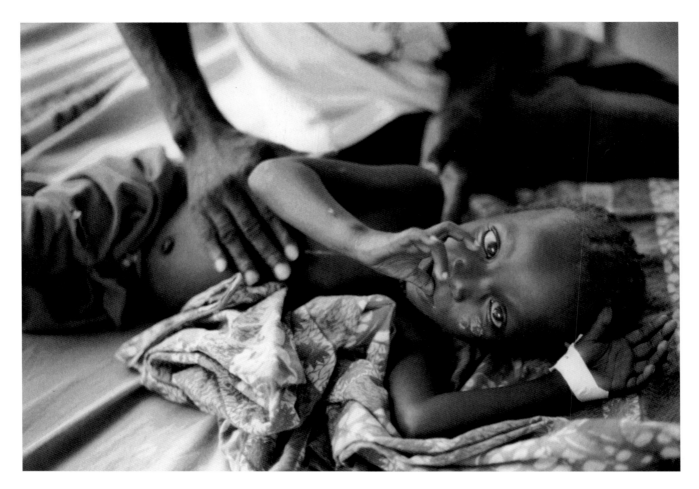

There are approximately 5000 disabled/victims of war in the camp. A considerable portion of them are war veterans, who have sought safety after their fighting days here in Kakuma. The camp has several programs for the disabled. Men take part in a wheelchair basketball game (left), as a reminder of the war and the land mines encountered lies in the foreground.

The International Rescue Committee oversees the delivery of all health care services in the camp. Set-up throughout the camp are several tents and clinics at the refugees' service. The Turkana are also provided with any request of health care assistance. This young boy (above) is a victim of another scourge on Africa, AIDS. His father said his son has become so ill, he no longer has the strength to cry.

The Turkana and refugee communities place much blame on each other for their suffering, but both actually help more than they harm each of the respective populations. The Turkana pay for the labor of willing refugees to assist in the harvesting of crops. Refugees also employ the Turkana to carry wood and do other tasks (left and above top). The Turkana are also free to use many resources of the camp that wouldn't be available without the presence of the refugees. Trade is also frequent between the two communities.

Two refugee children (above bottom) await the return of their parents from harvesting the Turkana millet field.

Water is provided for the refugees from several bore holes (wells) that have been drilled in the camp's nearby riverbed. The water is pumped to serving taps, which are evenly distributed throughout Kakuma.

Each day twenty-one liters of water are provided for each refugee. The waiting for and collecting of water is usually left as a task for the children. The water taps are in use at different times, which can make the process of obtaining water a long ordeal at times, depending on the lines.

Refugees receive plastic sheeting, blankets, kitchen sets, jerricans, and soap when they arrive at the camp (left). These items are replaced throughout the years. A refugee also receives 10 kgs of firewood per month. Clothing is provided by NGOs and distributed when available.

All of a family's basic necessities cannot be met by the UNHCR or by the NGOs. Often refugees will use their food rations to trade with other refugees for clothing or other items desired, but not provided. To ensure that refugee children get a meal each day, a special school feeding program was begun (above). It assured each child a serving of warm porridge on a daily basis.

The most important object to obtain as a refugee at Kakuma is a food ration card (above). One card is distributed to each head of household. The cards are an assurance of food, something that the refugees may not have had for years. They also act as a monitoring tool in order to keep up and provide camp statistics.

The World Food Programme supplies aid in the form of biweekly food distributions throughout the camp at various centers. The general feeding program provides a diet of approximately 2100 calories to each refugee daily, which includes cereals, oil, salt, pulses and soy blend.

Food, however, is occasionally withheld during the rainy season or windstorms, until conditions are safe for the distribution to take place. When violence breaks out or tensions are high within the community, for the safety of the refugees the food may not be released. Such instances can force families to live for several weeks on an already sparse two-week ration. There are no other food sources in the camp.

This mother (right) was distraught that she has only been given a half-ration for her family, due to a temporary lack of funding for the food program.

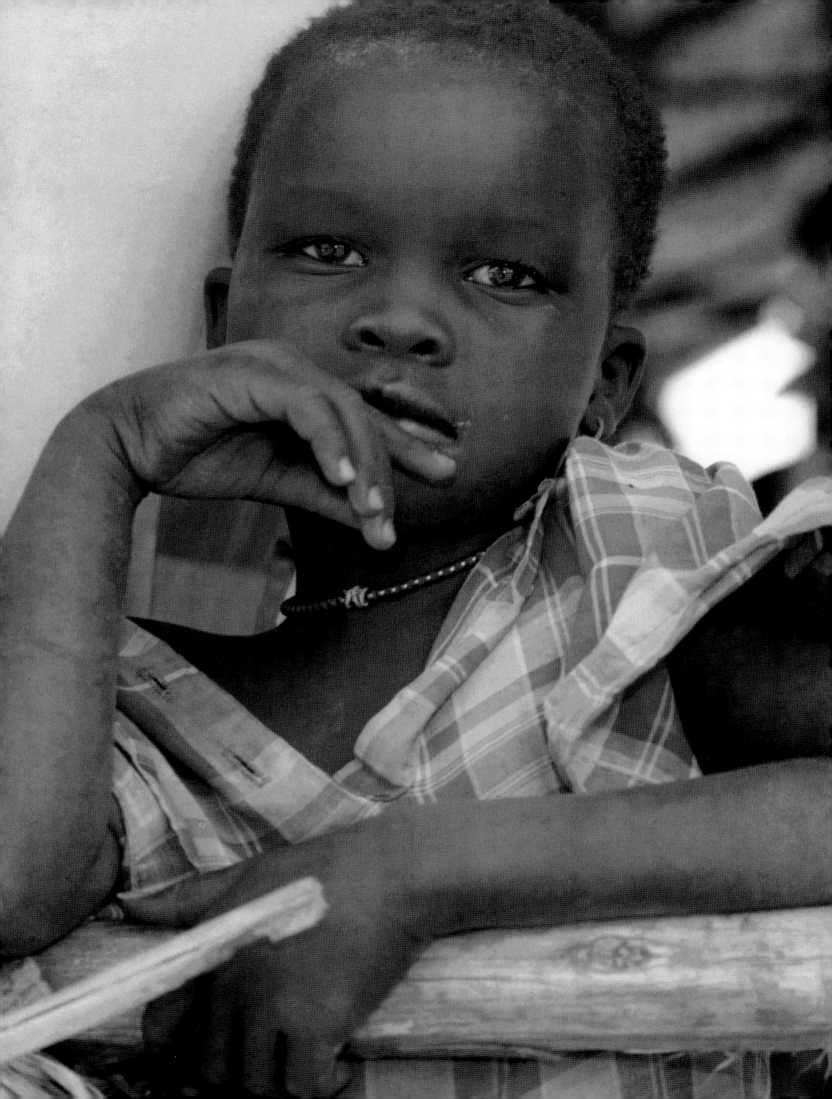

Some 75 miles later, the refugees reach Kakuma Refugee Camp from the Lokichokio transit center near the Kenya-Sudan border. The tightly packed refugees eagerly jump out of the truck and set foot on what is to be their new home.

They wait in a holding area for several weeks until additional housing is completed. The many temporary communal shelters are fenced and nothing more than concrete floors with corrugated metal roofs. They wait for the more permanent shelters of the camp constructed of mud bricks made by the refugees. Flattened tin cans from their rations are used as roofing material, covered with large plastic bags from rice and flour.

These modest huts provide little protection in the weather extremes of Turkana District, from dust and sandstorms to seasonal flooding. In 2001, nearly a quarter of the refugees—some 23,000 people—were left without shelter after four days of torrential rains.

Once in the camp, refugees are not allowed to leave. Refugee camps are intended as emergency housing until families return to their homelands, but in the case of Kakuma, this has almost become a settlement area due to the extraordinary length of the conflict in Sudan. Instead of weeks or months, some families have lived in the camp for two generations. By UNHCR and Kenyan mandate, the refugees cannot choose to assimilate into the host country's society and must remain in the camp until repatriation or relocation can be arranged for them. Depending on whether they believe it is safe enough, the refugees have the final decision to return to their home country or remain in the camp.

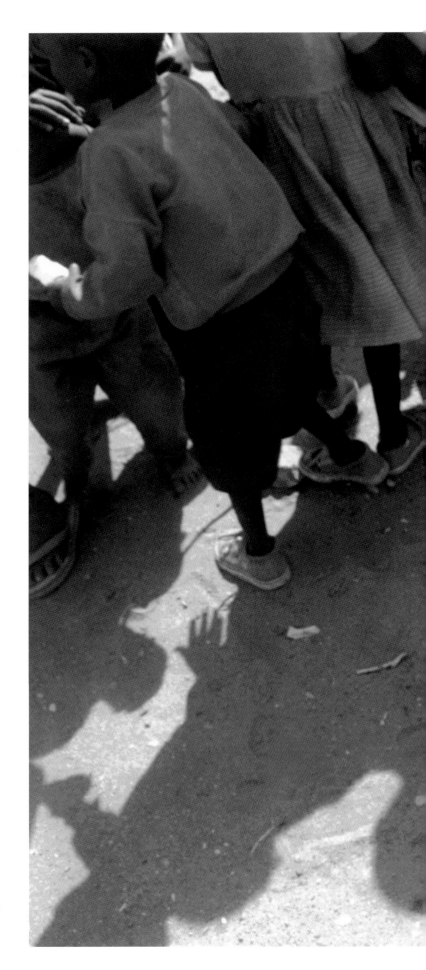

The same case does not apply to this young Sudanese boy. He has no comprehension of what the refugee camp is or what the truck is. All that he is concerned with is being in a new land, with new things, such as a camera and a foreigner—all first sightings in his short life. The boy gives off a gleaming smile as panic-stricken shadows jockey for position to board the truck behind him.

One last glance of uncertainty is given before this young refugee (above) boards the truck with her mother to Kakuma. In her pail is all that she owns; a comb, T-shirt and pen.

This little boy (right) falls in tears on the bags beneath him as he watches the truck pull away from the transit center, without him.

Sudanese refugee mothers (top left and above) share their anguish of lost husbands to the war. Most of the people at the camp are widows and their children or orphans. The task of protecting and raising their families on their own becomes overwhelming. Nearly all of the males over the age of fifteen are fighting for the liberation of their country or have been killed in combat.

The transit center is a difficult stop. Children are hungry and mothers can give them nothing. It is this feeling of helplessness that the wars in Kenya's border countries has placed on countless women.

A young girl lets off the slightest hint of a smile (lower left). But I can only wonder how, after hearing her story. The scar on her forehead is the reminder of a blow to the head from the butt of a gun, as she walked in on her mother being beaten by government-backed militia. This is a common act used to obtain information on SPLA whereabouts.

Two brothers run hand-in-hand to join the line for the truck (following pages). The realization has hit them: food and safety is now only hours away.

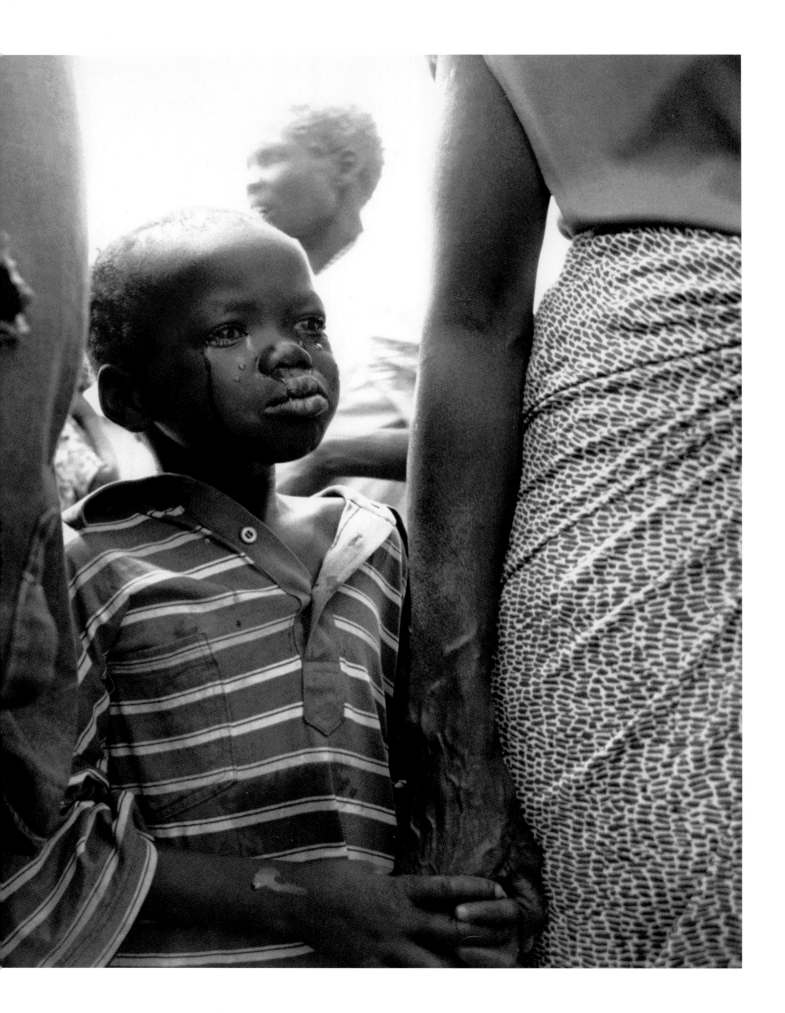

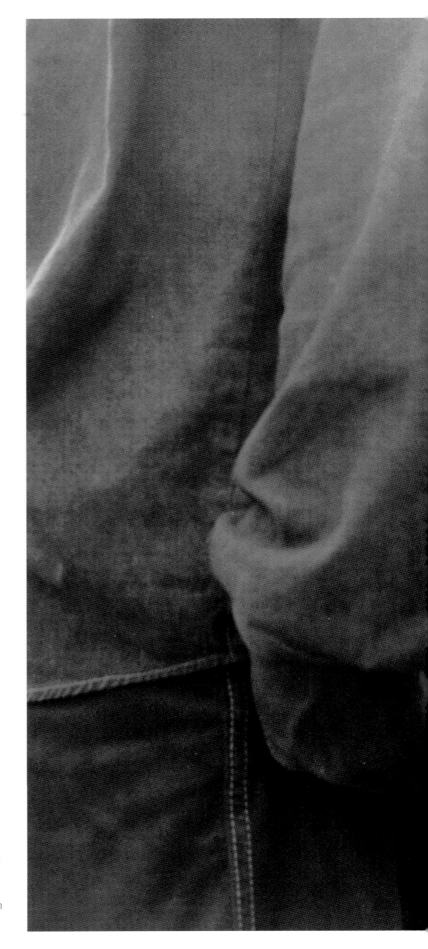

Throughout the madness of waiting to find who will board the truck to a place of safety and food, this young child shows strength far beyond her years. Scared and unsure of what is happening, she remains with a stoic expression not making one noise, as tears roll off her face one after the other. An entire generation has been born into the twenty-year ongoing war in Sudan.

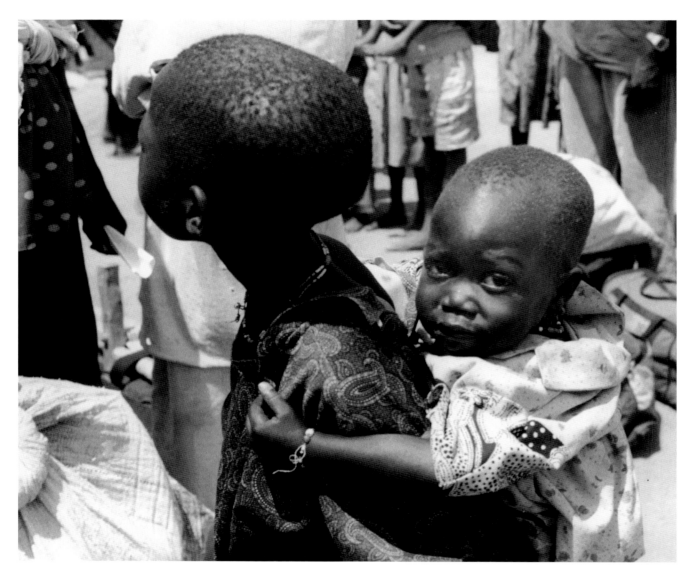

Sister grabs brother as bodies rush past. It is complete mayhem during the reading of the lists to confirm who will board the truck to Kakuma. Refugees hold on tightly to their bags and listen attentively for their names to be called.

A ghostly stare from eyes that witnessed horrible atrocities peer through the fence of the transit center in Lokichokio (previous page). This young girl fled her village in southern Sudan after repeated bombing campaigns by the government. She and other children await the arrival of the trucks from Kakuma to transport the new arrivals.

After a grueling several-day trek through desert and mountains, these three brothers (above) reached the transit center on the border. They watched as their father was shot in front of their eyes and fled their village with other family members. When asked how they survived, they responded, "Jesus, and my father. He was our angel. His spirit brought us to safety." The youngest brother was the first to point out his brother's shirt, which read, "May angels keep you night and day."

THE REFUGEES

It is a sanctuary for some of the world's most vulnerable people. Kakuma Refugee Camp is a safe haven to over 81,000 refugees. The camp was initially built for Sudanese refugees fleeing once-safe camps in Ethiopia. The military coup there of Colonel Mengistu Haile Mariam's government forced them to seek safety in a new land. After a journey back across war-ravaged South Sudan, these refugees found safety in Kenya's UNHCR Kakuma Refugee Camp. But the makeup of Kakuma's present population is not all Sudanese. There are nine different nationalities and over twenty ethnic groups. The majority though, about ninety percent, are coming from South Sudan. The small populations of other nationalities ranging from Somalis to Congolese have been transferred here as a result of protection issues and consolidation from other camps. Kakuma accepts a couple hundred to several thousand new Sudanese refugees each month, depending on the situation in South Sudan.

Reaching Kakuma is a long and difficult journey. Refugees must avoid the war zones and walk for days or months on end with little or no food, traversing mountains and desert. This brings them to southern Sudan and northern Kenya's border controlled by SPLA rebels, about 125 miles from Kakuma. It may be the last time that any of these refugees sets foot on his or her homeland of Sudan.

Only miles from the border crossing is the town of Lokichokio, Kenya. Here is the base for Operation Lifeline Sudan and other non-governmental organizations (NGO's) that work within South Sudan. Most importantly, though, Lokichokio is the UNHCR Transit Center. It is the first place of safety for many only thought of in dreams and the near conclusion of their exhausting journey. The transit center is nothing more that some fenced-in shelters and water pumps. Here new arrivals will be screened and processed in preparation for their transfer to Kakuma. Within only a couple days they will be transferred by truck to the camp, an hour's drive away.

The refugees are placed in another holding station at the camp where they may remain for up to several weeks. Little food or water is provided and only minimal shelter. From there they will go through another process of screening and interviews. Food ration cards will be distributed and, when materials to build a shelter are made available, they move into the community.

Kakuma Refugee Camp offers services from education and health to food and water distribution. Most importantly, however, it offers safety. These opportunities have attracted refugees from South Sudan in enormous numbers. There is concern for future refugees, as a result. Kakuma has expanded its camp numerous times and there is simply no more available land for these new refugees.

There is also the problem of South Sudan's infrastructure. Day by day, year by year, the war has taken its toll. The government of Kenya has stated that integration of the Sudanese refugee population into Kenyan society is not an option. Resettlement of such a large refugee population is unlikely. In time, they will have to return to South Sudan, but it will be to a deserted, destroyed land.

For nearly twenty years the conflict in Sudan has caused a mass exodus of southern Christians and animists who refuse to submit to Radical Islamic law. In acts of genocide, the northern radical Arab Islamic government has repeatedly made use of bombing campaigns on civilian settlements and hired militias to wipe out entire villages in the south. The slave trade thrives in Sudan, as young children are abducted from the south, then forced to convert to Islam and sold into slavery in the north. All of these are the causes and situations for which the South Sudanese are forced to flee their homeland.

There seems to be little hope for these incredible survivors, unless the international community gives more focus to the genocide and abuse of human rights in Sudan.

Three generations of a Turkana family (upper left) remain in their traditional ways. The young adolescent furthest right has a red soil substance spread across her chest. This signifies her availability to those in search of a wife.

In many indigenous cultures, song and dance hold great importance in their traditions and beliefs. Here a group of women (lower left) sing a song, calling on God to bring rain for their crops. Turkana children live a life filled with song and dance, playing from the early morning until late into the evening. Some schoolhouses are scattered throughout the community, but very few Turkana children are able to attend.

Traditionally Turkana women shave the sides of their heads, leaving a narrow strip of hair on top. This is usually braided. The practice gives them a defining look along with being very practical and cool in the extreme heat. When in mourning, as this woman is (above), a Turkana female will shave her entire head as a sign of respect and grief for the deceased.

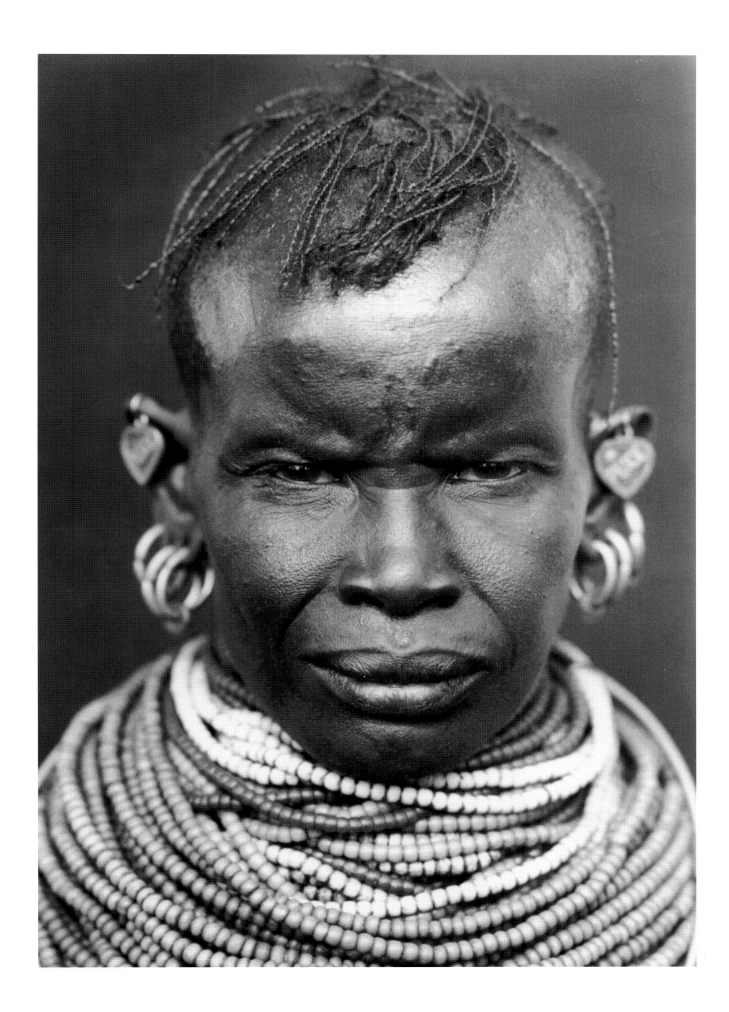

I asked some Turkana to bring the most special thing they have to be photographed with them (previous pages). One woman proudly displayed her plastic water pitcher, while another elderly woman brought her granddaughter.

Beauty flows endlessly in the Turkana culture. No trait is more recognizable or beautiful than a woman's necklace of beads (above, right and following pages). A mix of small and large, plastic and wooden, their beads carry significance far beyond the aesthetic.

They reveal a woman's wealth and social rank. Beads can be obtained from different events in life, such as childbirth, sickness or marriage. When a Turkana woman marries into a new family, she must disperse the beads that she owns throughout her new husband's family. The importance can be a deciding factor in a marriage. Women give great respect to their beads. For many, the beads will be their only possession in their lifetime.

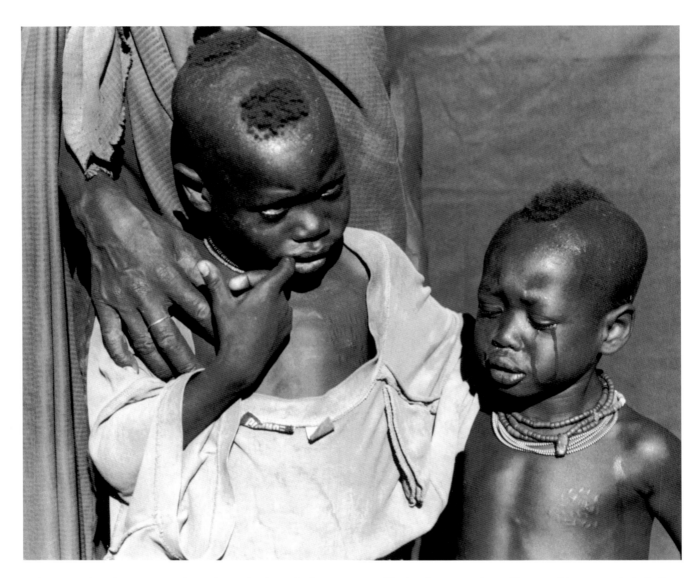

Turkana men (previous two pages) may have a herd numbering in the hundreds. The Turkana rarely kill their animals for meat, however. Nothing is more important to a Turkana man than his herd of cattle, providing both a link to the spiritual world and symbol of wealth in the temporal world. They are used as a dowry for marriage, even more coveted than money. Cattle skins and milk are also important aspects of the animal. But the greatest thing offered to the Turkana from their cattle is blood. A man will bleed his herd in rotation, no less than several weeks apart.

The consumption of blood is important for the Turkana far beyond traditional value. Due to the harsh environment there can be no reliable source of food. A Turkana person can go through weeks without food, surviving just by the nutrients gained in drinking blood. The cattle of a Turkana man are his responsibility to look after and protect. Rustling is frequent between different tribes in the region. This can result in a return raid or all out tribal war.

Scarification is commonly used by East African nomads, including the Turkana, as tribal identification and personal decoration (left). The patterns cut into the skin can represent various attributes from strength to beauty. It is an extremely painful process, but is quite frequent for both males and females as a ritual marking passage into puberty. Occasionally ash is rubbed into the cuts to increase the raised relief of the scar.

These brothers (above) share the mark of their family. Around each of their right nipples are scars left from cutting done to them at a young age. The scars reveal the clan to which they belong and their social status.

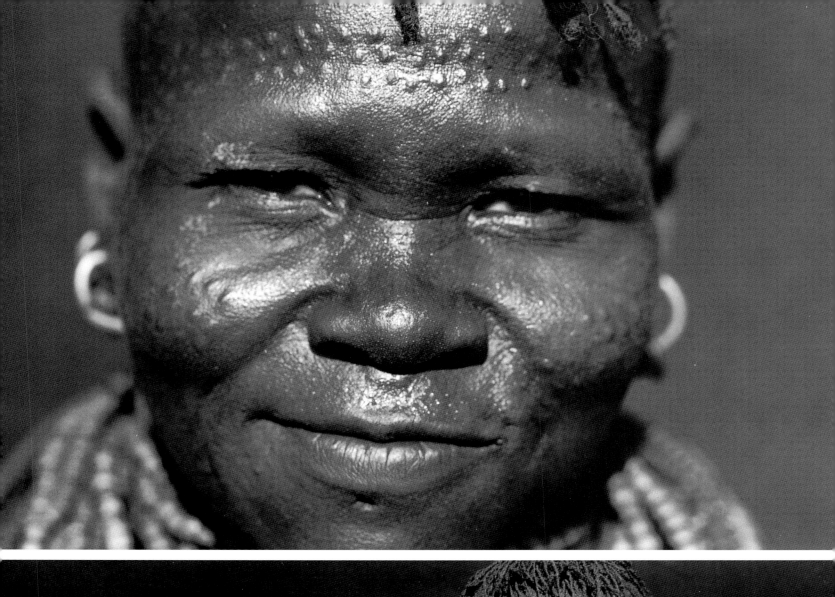

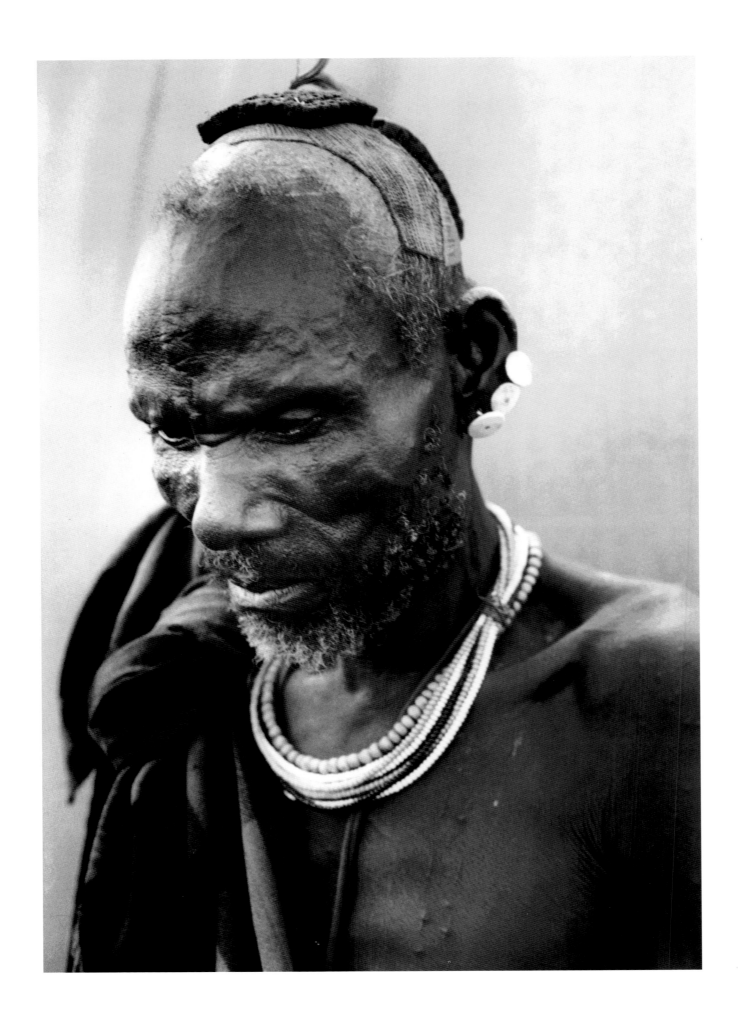

Turkana women have a life of watching the children (left) and performing chores, the most important of which is fetching water. It can take an entire day in the extreme equatorial heat to walk to the riverbed and back, carrying several gallons of water or more.

The Tarach River (above) remains dry throughout the majority of the year. It is the main source of water for many of the Turkana. Due to the arid conditions, those searching for water may have to dig several feet in order to obtain this precious natural resource.

A Turkana man (above) carries all essential life belongings with him. Around their right wrists, all Turkana men wear a bracelet made of sharpened steel. This is used in combat as well as for everyday tasks. A man often carries a walking cane along with a separate herding stick. Arguably their most prized possession is a Turkana man's stool (shown in left hand). This can be used to rest after a long day's journey following the herds and at night it is used as a pillow, to keep their heads off the ground while sleeping so that bugs don't crawl in their ears.

Although the Turkana life is one of resourcefulness and practicality, they hold a place for beautiful and elaborate clothing and jewelry. These men wear traditional caps and robes. This elder (right) displays a ball carved of ivory pierced through his lower lip.

THE TURKANA

A strong and mysterious people, the Turkana have sustained themselves in the brutal environment of north-western Kenya for thousands of years. Their ancestors are some of Africa's earliest inhabitants and believed to be one of the first peoples to walk the Earth. Here in Kakuma, they remained oblivious to the outside world. That was all about to change in July of 1992.

The warring nations that surrounded the Turkana's homeland set off a massive flood of refugees from all directions. Kakuma Refugee Camp was built in 1992 to accommodate the growing problems with refugees in Eastern Africa. The UNHCR and government of Kenya had decided that the best place for this camp would be on land in the remote northwest, the land of the Turkana.

When I began this project I had no comprehension that the Turkana even existed. There is almost no documentation of these forgotten peoples of the Rift Valley and it is quite simple to understand why: they have remained hidden, frozen in time, thriving with tradition, untouched.

The Turkana are a mainly pastoralist people, moving from one place to another in order to feed their herds. The most common animals that they keep are goats. Goats are able to survive in the harsh region's environment with little water and grazing land. Cattle and camels are a few of the other animals they herd.

Since the introduction of the refugee camp, this once isolated people has been forced to co-habitate with an outside community. Though the camp offers the Turkana some medical attention and educational opportunities, it is difficult for them to understand. While the Turkana suffer and starve, these new refugee visitors on their homeland receive food and water. The Turkana question why it is not they who are being assisted. Some are now being forced out of their traditional ways, leaving their villages for jobs in far away city factories.

My first journey to a Turkana village is one that I will never forget. The villages are located on the outskirts of the camp. The trek took several hours of navigating through dry riverbeds. Making our way around scorched, cracked earth, even the Land Rover got stuck in several ruts, a couple of dried out riverbeds and died once on the way. The transportation issues were the least of my problems. The temperature in the car must have been hovering near the century mark. I hit my head on the window numerous times and even meet the ceiling of the truck once, doing wonders for my headache. All of this, though, seemed minute compared to the conflict brewing in my gut. The basic diet at the camp mess where I ate was goat soup. There was the occasional fish or mashed potatoes, but if you couldn't handle the goat soup staple you would starve. The bumps, the heat, my headache and my stomach pain would make you think that such a trek would be unbearable, but that was far from the truth. I wouldn't have wished to be anywhere else in the world.

We made our way past gun-toting Turkana men—the area has become infamous for its banditry—past the long lines of Turkana women balancing large buckets of water on their heads, past the old Turkana men playing games and gossiping under the shade of a tree. We began passing small groupings of two or three huts, a sign that we were near our destination.

When I arrived at the village, it was far beyond any dream of mine. The entire village—old women, men and children—stood in a large group singing and dancing in welcome to me. Usually, in moments like this, one's heart would be racing. It was odd, though, for me. I felt my heart seem to stop. I would be the first westerner ever to set foot in this village. Was I doing the right thing to even be here? I didn't want to disrupt their traditional ways; I wanted only to document those aspects of their lives for posterity.

I spent my days photographing the Turkana in the burning sun. Sometimes a stray hand would appear in the lens or an inquisitive face would make its way into the frame. Others kept their distance, fearing the camera was a weapon. Crowds of curious onlookers watched as friends and family had their pictures taken for the first time.

INTRODUCTION

When I met Daniel first visiting the dusty refugee camp of Kakuma, I did not realize that he was only fifteen years old. He impressed me by his maturity and determination. He quickly integrated into the community of aid workers and interacted effortlessly with refugees. Daniel also wove extremely valuable relations in the social fabric of the local Turkana population. Honestly, after two days, I did not need to worry about his well-being and security, two of the major concerns in that part of the world.

Most of all, I admired Daniel's human qualities. In this book, he describes his "first love" as "a sea of suffering humanity, mud shelters and plastic sheeting, hungry stomachs and heavy hearts." These are profound words by a heartwarming young man and capture the stark realities of life in a refugee camp.

Daniel's book is a wonderful pictorial essay of human struggle for the survival of values against man-made and natural catastrophes. It is also an extraordinary tale of generosity towards those who flee war, misery, intolerance and hatred. It is his profound cry during a time of innocence, calling for humanity, humility and consciousness. But above all, it is a tribute to both the refugee populations' courage and resolve in the face of hardships and human suffering—and to the warmth and generosity of the receiving community.

I know the Turkana very well, having lived amongst them for nearly three and a half years. Their nobility will always evoke very pleasant feelings in my heart and their strength will forever shine in my memories. They belong to those people whose simplicity, kindness and spirit merit recounting all over the world. Turkana is a land where the human species may have originated, and its inhabitants are tireless wanderers who exemplify respect for the dignity and values of others.

Oh, if all mankind were like the Turkana, probably the world would have faced less disaster. They should not be "the last Mohicans" of East Africa! And, Daniel's book aims to ensure this is not so.

The bare, semiarid and least developed Kenyan district of Turkana is an extraordinary land of hospitality for refugees, particularly South Sudanese, who are fleeing their war-ravaged homelands in search of international protection. South Sudanese, these other heroes of African pride and values, are remarkable human beings—trustworthy and trustful of friendship—who do not understand why the terrible plague of violence has afflicted them for so long.

I have also known the wonderful peoples of South Sudan very well, for I have felt that I have myself become a Dinka, a Nuer, an Equatorian, a Cordofane and a refugee from their welcome of me into their lives. Even as refugees, they are always giving more than they receive. I will never forget the hopeful eyes of Sudan's "Lost Boys" when I first met with them in their "villages" in Kakuma Refugee Camp. The terrible flight, suffering and losses that they endured never diminished their belief in a better future.

Daniel's book is a remarkable appeal for the safeguard of Turkana and South Sudanese traditions—and, indeed, a reminder of the plight of refugees everywhere in the world, who are the "voiceless" amongst the inhabitants of the Earth.

Saber Azam, PhD
Deputy Director, Office of the Special Representative
   of the United Nations Secretary General for Kosovo
Former Deputy Special Envoy for South-East Europe
   and past Head of Operations in East and West Africa,
   United Nations High Commissioner for Refugees
PRISTINA, KOSOVO

ACKNOWLEDGMENTS

I am forever indebted to the thousands of indigenous Turkana and refugees of Kakuma who opened their hearts and lives in trust to me. It was you who pushed and sustained me throughout this entire journey. Your resilience and will to survive have affected me beyond what words can describe. With all of my heart I give you my deepest gratitude and thanks.

This project would not have been possible without logistical and moral support from the United Nations High Commissioner for Refugees. Many thanks to all who assisted from UNHCR Nairobi: Alberto Carlos Cabeia Chys, Paul Stromberg and Surasak Satawiriya. Many thanks to all of Kakuma's NGO's and their staffs: Don Bosco, World Food Programme, International Committee of the Red Cross, International Rescue Committee, World Vision Kenya, GTZ and Lutheran World Federation.

Special thanks to all UNHCR Kakuma staff for your steadfast assistance. You and Kakuma have become a second home for me. Firstly, I thank Dr. Saber Azam, UNHCR Deputy Special Envoy and former camp director at Kakuma. How you gave so much respect to a blurry-eyed fifteen-year-old with a camera is beyond my comprehension. Without your assistance and willingness to help in the beginning, this project would be nothing. To Kakuma Director Kofi Mable, who continued that same respect and support, your help is greatly appreciated. Thank you to Ben Ngaira, Kakuma security officer, for your friendship and for keeping me alive.

"Odindo," my good friend! David Odindo you have become one of my best friends. Your dedication to assisting refugees amazes me. Thank you for all that you have given. From help inside the camp to our late-night chats outside the mess, you are always in my thoughts. To my great drivers Dominic and Jermano, for going far beyond your duty to assist me, my thanks.

Many thanks to Daniel Lokuyen Ekaran for your relentless work with me and the Turkana communities. You have my deepest appreciation, for without your willingness to share your world I would have never been allowed into the lives of the Turkana. A special thanks to all the Turkana of villages Natiir 1 and Natiir 2.

My gratitude goes to all close to home who have been able to put up with me throughout this project—especially my mother, Gail Martinson, and Salvador Martinez; my father, William Yang, and Joua Yang; my lovely sister Anna and the rest of my family and friends who provided me with such tremendous support—especially Sara Duerr for keeping me smiling. Thanks to Teresa Loeffler for all your generous help and to Angie Harper who pushed me always to search for the truth. If not for Issara Yangsirisuk and family's support, this project would not have even begun.

Many thanks to Dick and Debbie Bancroft, my extended family, for your guidance as I continue on this journey.

I express my solidarity with the American Indian Movement, Ejército/Frente Zapatista Liberación Nacional and the Sudanese Peoples' Liberation Army/Movement. Freedom for Leonard Peltier. Freedom for Palestine and Tibet. I am thankful for personal inspiration from Crazy Horse, Emiliano Zapata, Ernesto "Che" Guevara and Nelson Mandela.

And I extend my appreciation for photographic inspiration to James Nachtwey and Edward S. Curtis. Thank you to film director Oliver Stone, producer Dan Halsted and the crew for assistance in Kakuma during your filming.

A special note of gratitude must go to His Holiness the Dalai Lama, his staff in Dharamsala and the government of Tibet in Exile for helping this work to find its way into the hands of His Holiness.

Finally, to my publisher and editor Bonnie Hayskar, you have become a mentor and more importantly a great friend—I thank you from the bottom of my heart. In memory of grandfather Gaze Yang, I hope that I have honored your name and thank you for sharing your wisdom.

into perspective.

I started to think about recording my experiences in a book as a way to bring attention to what was going on in this part of the world. "Was it possible that I could save the indigenous or solve the refugee crisis in East Africa? Could I stop the suffering and conflict?" It is very unlikely that any book alone could do all that. But someday this book might fall into the hands of someone who can.

Throughout this project I have been asked the question, "Will there ever be any hope for the people of South Sudan?" To this inquiry, I can offer only one response. It is a story from my last visit to Kakuma. The day was Easter Sunday 2001, a holy day for the Christian refugees in Kenya who, in their homeland, would not be able to practice their religion. During their Easter celebrations, fighting broke out within the refugee camp. Gunfire from AK-47's echoed through the deserted streets. The fighting was a direct result of inter-factional disputes within the Sudanese Peoples Liberation Army (SPLA) across the border in Sudan. News of the disputes had reached the camp and turned the place that was once a refuge into a war zone similar to the ones the refugees had fled.

The day was filled with rock-throwing, spear-fighting and the release of sporadic gunfire. Women and children who were caught in the middle of the fighting fled to one of the camp's churches. Hundreds of refugees crammed together into the protection of the tiny building. I made my way to the church compound to gather accounts of the fighting and saw that these refugees had essentially become internally displaced in their own refugee camp. Many of them thought this was ironic. I went through the church talking to children and women. All were distraught and crying.

One little girl in the corner caught my eye. Most of the refugees in the church were with family members or at least acquaintances, huddling together after the horrific fighting, but not this girl. She sat alone in the corner, faced towards the wall, tracing her fingers in the dusty floor. I approached her and gently tapped her on the shoulder. As she turned to face me a tear fell from her weathered face. I sat down next to her and asked how she was doing. She replied with the customary, "Fine, thank you" that I received from almost every refugee child at Kakuma. Then more tears began to slip from her eyes. I asked where her family

was and she began to cry more.

She placed her hand on my knee so I knew that I was not imposing on her. I sat with her until the tears subsided. It was then that I looked down at what she was drawing with her finger on the dusty floor. It appeared to be an outline of Sudan with a village scene in the middle. I told her I liked her picture and asked if she had family there. She told me that her mother was shot to death in front of her for not agreeing to go with government forces.

The tears began to form again. I tried to change the subject. "What is your picture of? Is it the 'New Sudan'?" The New Sudan is the term given to the parts of South Sudan controlled by the SPLA forces. She quickly replied, "No!" It was an odd reply, one that only someone opposed to the SPLA would respond; even more odd because almost all South Sudanese were in support of the SPLA.

I wondered if she had anyone else in her family and she told me about her brother. As her tears came again, she explained in broken English how she had just seen him being stoned to death right before fleeing to the church. It then occurred to me, she had gone through witnessing the murder of her mother by the government-backed radical Muslim militias of the north, and now had just witnessed the murder of her brother by her very own people. I sat there speechless next to her on the cold cement floor and, for the first time in my many trips to Kakuma, felt tears of my own welling up.

Then the young girl turned to me and smiled through her sadness. She pointed to the dusty floor and her picture and said, "My picture is to be of a land with no hatred and with no death. In this land families can stay together and they can be happy. Everyone can eat and no one will be killed. Children can go to school and live in peace. All tribes can live together, all colors and religions together. No one will kill each other anymore."

I asked her how this could happen. She told me that she had a plan. I asked if she would share it with me. She said it was a secret, but not to worry. So I'll let you decide whether there is hope left or not. For me, though, a little girl who has lost all family but not hope, is hope enough for me.

Daniel Cheng Yang
SAINT PAUL, MINNESOTA USA

twenty years the south has resisted, but at great cost. How was I to create awareness and change in a land halfway across the world, while I was still not even old enough to legally drive a car?

After weeks and months of phone calls and emails, I was granted permission by the United Nations High Commissioner for Refugees (UNHCR) to visit a refugee camp near the border of Sudan and Kenya. The camp was a safe haven for Sudanese refugees fleeing their war-torn homeland. The camp was called Kakuma.

In the fall of 1999 I made my first trip to Kakuma. It was on that trip that I found my first love. I had heard my friends talking of their first love and how they knew from the moment they saw her that she would be their first. This happened the same way for me. She did not have blond hair or beautiful blue eyes. She was a sea of suffering humanity, mud shelters and plastic sheeting, hungry stomachs and heavy hearts. Her name is Kakuma and not a day or night passes without me thinking of her.

I wasn't sure what I was doing there at the time. I had no thoughts of writing a book or giving lectures. I simply wanted to immerse myself in the refugees' suffering to find ways to ease it. The trip was to learn firsthand what these people had experienced. When I reached Kakuma, 500 miles by plane from Nairobi, the first signs of suffering were revealed to me not by the refugees but by the indigenous population of the Turkana.

On the land where the Turkana have lived for centuries is where the United Nations erected a camp for the vulnerable refugees seeking sanctuary. Here, two groups of Africa's forgotten peoples were forced together in a dueling struggle for survival. The Turkana have persevered for many hundreds of years in this remote land that has nearly no water or vegetation. It is difficult for the indigenous communities of the Turkana to witness the aid and assistance handed out to the refugees, while they live in absolute poverty and deprivation. This has created conflict between the two communities, an unfortunate situation of trying to survive, each in their respective struggles.

The opportunity of being allowed into the world of the Turkana is something I could have never imagined—to document a people who, in most cases, have never had contact with the outside world. Yet, while traveling to remote villages I carried with me some guilt. I did not want to exploit their ancient culture. I had to constantly remind myself that my goal was to ease suffering. Still, at times I wondered if it was correct to disturb their tranquility, even if it was to help their people. This was an issue I was forced to face throughout the project. How far was too far? When was enough, enough? Should I photograph a dead newborn? Were the ribs of a starving child important to the project? What about a man shot in the back of the head as his lifeless body lay in the sand? I determined that it was of absolute importance to document all of these instances. As soon as one begins to ignore any aspect of suffering, the total truth may not be revealed.

After my first trip to Kakuma in 1999 I made several more solo trips back to what has now become my second home. I found it odd that in a land on the complete opposite side of the globe from where I live is a place where I feel most comfortable—a short and stocky Asian kid walking through a forest of tall and skinny pitch-black Africans. Kakuma was my first love and the people my passion. The pieces eventually fell into place and I realized that the most significant way for me to create awareness was by documenting the struggles of the great people of Kakuma, both the refugees and the indigenous. At times I thought this venture was impossible for a simple boy to find financial backing, logistical support and a publisher; then I remembered the extreme suffering and obstacles conquered by the people of Kakuma and it seemed to always put things

So, too, are the other 40 million refugees around the world and their stories of survival. Refugees are businessmen, farmers and doctors. They are grandmothers, fathers and sisters. They are no different than you and me.

I remember back to 1994, seeing a young naive boy in front of the television flipping through various afternoon cartoons. He was searching for something, something but he didn't know what. During a commercial break, the boy set aside his snack of cookies and milk and focused intently on the screen in front of him. He saw mutilated bodies, hundreds of dead children piled on top of each other and lines of thousands of people fleeing. His young mind knew this was not a new television show, movie or commercial.

Then the voice of a local news anchor began speaking over the horrific images, "Tonight on the five o'clock news, civil war in Rwanda." The anchor continued to talk of other stories—the weather and the beginning of the new baseball season—but the young boy's mind was fixated on the sight of the atrocities being committed in this new country to him, named Rwanda.

The young child continued watching TV until the familiar introduction to the local news began. Where was the story on this place called Rwanda? He wanted to find out what those gruesome images were. It was not to be. There was an important press conference of a local sports player, which was of much greater significance than the conflict in the tiny African country of Rwanda. The boy turned off the TV in wonderment. I was that boy.

The genocide of Rwanda was a turning point in my life. I had never been there. I didn't know anyone from there. But what I learned in the weeks, months and years to come after the genocide of 1994 has pushed me to strive to create awareness of and aid for the millions of refugees internationally—the world's most vulnerable peoples. Rwanda experienced nearly one million deaths from a systematic plan of massacre intended to rid the country of an entire population. It was a genocide in which the dead grew at nearly three times the rate of the Jews during the Holocaust. Yet no one was speaking of it. The genocide went along ignored, taking backseat to Hollywood scandals and sports scores. I promised myself at that time that I would do whatever I could to assure something like this would never happen again, or at least not be ignored.

In 1999, it was time for me to follow through on my promise. I was fifteen years old and a freshman in high school. I had continued to study the conditions in Africa and had become very concerned about the conflict in the Sudan. Over the past twenty years, the war between the north and the south in that country has taken the lives of over two million victims in South Sudan—almost one out of every five South Sudanese has died as a result of the war. Four million South Sudanese have been forced to flee their homes and become internally displaced—the largest internally displaced population in the world in 2002—and 500,000 have become refugees in neighboring countries.

The north-south political and religious split dates back to Sudan's colonial days under the control of the United Kingdom and Egypt. Independence was granted in 1956, but the country was already split between the Arab Muslim north and indigenous animist and Black Christian south.

In recent years, upheaval has been attributed to the Radical Arab Islamic regime of Khartoum. Sudan's ruling National Islamic Front (NIF) seized power in a 1989 military coup that overthrew an elected government and General Omar Hassan al-Bashir became president.

"The government continues to exert control by limiting free assembly, association and speech of independent civil society, including human rights monitoring organizations, and by silencing its critics through a variety of means including politically motivated charges that often carry the death penalty, " according to Human Rights Watch. "A civil war in the southern part of the country for more than sixteen years has resulted in government and rebel abuses against civilians including militia and army looting of food supplies, killing and injuring civilians (and, by government forces and militia, kidnaping of civilians for slavery purposes), burning of homes, and disruption of relief efforts, causing the displacement of hundreds of thousands and creating major famine."

Even before Bashir, the Khartoum regime had begun in the early 1980's to implement a scorched-earth policy, bombing the south and enslaving the southern women and children. The denial of food became an effective mass weapon to destroy its opposition. The Khartoum government demanded that the animist and Christian south convert to Islamic law, practice the Muslim faith, speak and write only in Arabic and give up its oil-rich lands. For nearly

PREFACE

As far back as I can remember into my childhood, stories of fleeing have always surrounded me. Tales of dodging bombs, navigating through dense jungles and hiding in caves took the place of "The Three Little Pigs" and other conventional bedtime stories. I wouldn't have had it any other way. The spillover effects of the Vietnam War caused my grandfather's family to flee their village in the mountains of Laos. They joined a massive flood of refugees into Thailand, in hopes of escaping persecution and death. My father, a young boy at the time—very close to my age now—recalls with vivid detail the atrocities he and others faced as refugees. He has always taken the opportunity to remind me of the suffering around the world that too many of us fail to acknowledge.

One particular story I remember him telling has stayed with me. The group of refugees that my father and his family were fleeing with had reached the final stages of trekking through carnage to reach freedom and safety. It had been several weeks of constant walking, with next to nothing to eat. As they quietly passed through the jungle night, they heard sounds coming from the bushes. Fearing that it was a group of soldiers that had been hunting them since fleeing their village, all sat motionless and quiet on the damp jungle floor.

Then, through the bushes came not a column of armed soldiers, but a child. It was a young girl who had fled with a group of refugees that had left just days before my father's. Her mother had fallen ill and could not keep up with the rest of the group. Fearing that the entire group would be slaughtered if they all remained while the woman recovered, they had decided there was no choice but to move on. Only one person was brave enough to stay by her side—her daughter.

The group tried to convince the little girl to come with them, even her mother pleaded for her to leave. Fearing an imminent death the group went on, leaving the two behind. The girl covered her mother with the only possession they had—a torn, thin blanket. She sat next to her for two days until the third morning when her mother did not wake from her sleep.

The young child was lost. Lost in the middle of the jungle. Lost in the middle of a civil war. Lost in the middle of life and death. When she approached my father's group she had only enough strength to crawl and beg for their assistance. Every young child in the group already carried an even younger child on his back. All the adults carried with them just enough food for the group to survive. No one had the strength to carry the girl. All they could do was share the little food they had with her and move on. They were forced to leave the child behind, alone, to eventually meet the same fate as her mother.

My father told me of how distraught this made him feel as a young boy seeing another young person no different than himself have to go through such great suffering. There was nothing he or the group could do but continue with the struggle for their own survival.

Several weeks went by. Many in my father's group had died from starvation and disease; some by bullets and others from land mines. Babies were washed away from their families in river crossings—often their mothers met the same fate, choosing to save their child or put an end to their own misery. My father managed to survive all of the agony around him and months after he first fled his village in Laos, he reached a refugee camp in Thailand.

While waiting in line for registration he felt a tug on his pant leg. There stood the very same girl they had left behind, believing that her death was inevitable. The girl told my father how the food they had shared with her had given her strength. One night she had heard shots being fired and realized it was her last chance for survival. She began running—bloodied feet racing across muddy jungle floors. Weeks later she arrived in the camp. It was miracle.

FOREWORD

The underlying theme of this book is human dignity. Every member of the human family has an equal and inalienable right to liberty, not just in terms of political freedom, but also at the fundamental level of freedom from fear and want. Sadly, today, despite all the reports of movement towards greater freedom and democracy in many parts of the world, the number of genuine refugees is, if anything, increasing. Individuals and groups on nearly every continent are daily fleeing their homes in fear of persecution because of their race, religion, nationality, social identity or political opinion. Others are fleeing merely in search of food and shelter.

In this book of photographs, Daniel Cheng Yang has documented people who, fleeing violence in their own lands, have sought the protection of the Kakuma Refugee Camp in northwest Kenya. At the same time, his eye has also been caught by the indigenous people of the region still pursuing their ages old way of life against great odds.

As a Tibetan who has spent the best part of his life in exile, I recognize the trouble these people face. As a refugee there is an ever-present sense of insecurity, for even though you may be relatively free you do not live in your own land. It is immensely difficult to cope with the loss of rights and abilities that most of us simply take for granted.

Although Daniel Cheng Yang is still very young I am impressed by the maturity he has shown not only in recognizing these peoples' plights, but also in identifying a way he can help them by simply documenting their experience and publishing it in this book. I am always especially encouraged when I come across such kindness and warm-heartedness towards others in one so young. I feel it bodes well for humanity's future, making me confident that this new century will see a more friendly, more caring and more understanding human family evolving on this planet.

The Dalai Lama
Thekchen Choeling
DHARAMSALA, INDIA

To the suffering, persecuted and oppressed—
and those who fight for them

International Standard Book Number
1-929165-50-1

Library of Congress Cataloguing-in-Publication Data

Yang, Daniel Cheng, 1983-
    Kakuma, Turkana : dueling struggles : Africa's forgotten peoples / Daniel Cheng Yang.
            p. cm.
Summary: Documents the way of life of the indigenous Turkana of Kenya, an ancient pastoralist
people, and the over 81,000 refugees of civil war in the Sudan and other East African nations who
have fled to Kakuma Refugee Camp on Turkana land since 1992.
        ISBN 1-929165-50-1 (hardcover : alk. paper)
        1. Sudan--History--Civil War, 1983---Refugees--Pictorial works. 2. Kakuma (Kenya : Refugee
camp)--Pictorial works. 3. Refugees--Sudan--Pictorial works. 4. Turkana (African people)--Social
conditions--Pictorial works. 5. Kenya--Ethnic relations--Pictorial works. [1. Sudan--History--Civil
War, 1983---Refugees--Pictorial works. 2. Kakuma (Kenya : Refugee camp)--Pictorial works. 3.
Refugees--Kenya. 4. Turkana (African people) 5. Kenya--Ethnic relations. 6. Youths' writings.] I.
Title.

DT157.672 .Y36 2002
962.404--dc21

                                                                    2001008459

Title page: Located in the northwest of Kenya, the Turkana region's harsh, dry environment
is the cause of much suffering for its people. Vegetation of any kind and rain to assist
crops are rare. It becomes a struggle to find something as simple as wood for shelter
and cooking. While there are some trees and shrubs in the villages, they are preserved for
shade. The Turkana returning to the village have walked several days to find wood.

Printed in China through Phoenix Offset

Published in the United States of America

P A N G A E A
www.pangaea.org info@pangaea.org

2002

TURKANA
Africa's Forgotten Peoples

DANIEL CHENG YANG

with foreword by
HIS HOLINESS THE DALAI LAMA

and introduction by
SABER AZAM

PANGAEA

SAINT PAUL